On an Island in the Bay

TEXT AND PHOTOGRAPHS BY

Patricia Mills

NORTH-SOUTH BOOKS / NEW YORK

FOR MY PARENTS

Published in the United States and Canada
by North-South Books Inc., New York.

Library of Congress Cataloging-in-Publication Data is available.
ISBN 1-55858-333-5 (trade edition)
ISBN 1-55858-334-3 (library edition)

Designed by Marc Cheshire
1 3 5 7 9 TB 10 8 6 4 2
1 3 5 7 9 LB 10 8 6 4 2
Printed in Belgium

For information on efforts being made to restore the productivity
and preserve the beauty of the Chesapeake Bay contact:

Alliance for the Chesapeake
6600 York Road, Suite 100, Baltimore, MD 21212
(410) 377-6270   (800) 662-2747

Chesapeake Bay Foundation, Inc.
162 Prince George Street, Annapolis, MD 21401
(410) 268-8816   (800) 445-5572

ON AN ISLAND IN THE BAY

AUTHOR'S NOTE

I first read about the remote islands of the Chesapeake Bay in a newspaper article several years ago. Immediately fascinated, I wanted to learn more about these isolated, distinct, and fragile communities. Three years ago I made my first trip to one of the islands, where villages dotted with crab houses and workboats rest in a great brackish marsh. Since then I have often visited the Chesapeake islands, exploring the villages, creeks, marshes, and shoreline. Out on the main bay I enjoyed crabbing and oyster dredging with the independent and resilient watermen.

The photographs in this book do not depict the life of any one island, but constitute a blend of several fishing communities. I want to thank the watermen and their families who graciously allowed me to photograph them and hear their stories of the bay.

For decades, environmentalists have been concerned about the effects of development, pollution, and overharvesting on this treasured estuary. Believing that the first spark of passion for protecting the environment arises from experiencing the joy of nature's glory, I created this book to encourage children to celebrate the splendor of this threatened environment and the dwindling traditional life on the islands in the bay.

In the very early morning

on an island in the bay,

cool gentle waves lap the shore

while watermen make ready

to follow the water.

Along creeks and coves,

amidst faintly golden grasses bending with the breeze,

mallards quack and dabble.

Diamondback terrapins bask on the banks.

A tall egret silently scouts the marsh for fish.

Here and there, young crabbers in low boats

net the beautiful swimmers, the blue crabs.

Fishermen cast lines

and catch rockfish.

Pale and delicate rose mallows gleam in the noonday sun,

low clouds drift by in blueness,

and the sea rushes to the shore on an island in the bay.

Out on the broad open waters, past the old shipwreck

and the lovely hammocks of loblolly pine,

round the grand lighthouse,

watermen in white-hulled workboats hook and pull crab pots.

All day watermen pull and haul crab pots.

Skipjacks of a time gone by sail along

harvesting oysters.

As the dark of day nears,

the last boats head back to the busy docks and crab shanties of home.

And the waters meet the sands of an island in the bay.